CW00432326

THE PRIMAR_ ENGLISH DIRECTORY

WRITTEN AND COMPILED BY MARK CHATTERTON MA (OXON)

CONTENTS

MW EDUCATIONAL

PARTS OF SPEECH

All words in the English language have a part to play in any sentence and each word in a sentence is a part of speech. The main parts of speech (or **word classes** as they are now called) are:- nouns, verbs, pronouns, determiners, adjectives, adverbs, prepositions and conjunctions. (This section also deals with interjections and articles). Each part of speech is discussed in detail below:-

NOUNS -   A **noun** is the name of a person, animal, place or thing.
Examples - **Jane** is a person; **rabbit** is an animal; **hospital** is a place; **table** is a thing.

In <u>most</u> cases, a noun is anything that you can see around you.

Nouns are given different names according to their particular functions:-

A COMMON NOUN is the <u>general</u> name of a thing or a person.
Examples - man, lion, village, pencil, etc.

A PROPER NOUN is the name of a particular <u>person</u> or <u>place</u> or <u>thing</u>.
Examples - Susan is a proper noun of a named **person**.
Liverpool is a proper noun of a named **place**.
September is a proper noun of a named **thing**.

Note: Proper nouns usually begin with a capital letter as they are **naming words**.

A COLLECTIVE NOUN is the name of a particular <u>group of things</u>.
Examples - a *swarm* of bees, a *chest* of drawers,   the football *team*.

Note: Collective nouns are usually singular and do not have capital letters

AN ABSTRACT NOUN is the name of something that <u>cannot</u> be seen, touched, tasted, heard or smelt.
Examples - a lie, pleasure, a thought, reason, concentration, forgiveness, etc.

Note: many abstract nouns have these endings (or suffixes):-

-ion:- illusion/motion   **-ity**:- equality   **-ment**:- department   **-ness**:- goodness

A CONCRETE NOUN is the name of something that <u>can be</u> seen, touched, tasted, heard or smelt. (It is the complete opposite of an abstract noun).
Examples - bus, chocolate, hair, etc.

Singular / Plural

Nouns can be either **singular** (one) or **plural** (more than one). To make a singular noun into a plural noun you usually add -s or -es to the end of the singular noun. This is called **inflection**. e.g. friend friends   bus buses
Usually if the noun ends in -ch -s -sh x or z you add **-es**, other wise you add **-s**.

There are some **exceptions** to this general rule and these are set out below:
If the noun ends in **y** and has a vowel before it you add -s:-   boy boy**s**
If the noun ends in y and has a consonant before it you remove the y and add -**ies**:-   e.g.   lady lad**ies**   county count**ies**
If the noun ends in **o** you add an **s**:-   e.g.   halo halo**s**
Exceptions to this rule add -**es**:   e.g.   hero hero**es**   potato potato**es**
Similarly, most nouns that end in **f** just have -s added to them to make them plurals:- e.g. chief chief**s**   roof roof**s**
Exceptions to this rule remove the **f** and have -**ves** added to the ending:-
e.g.   leaf lea**ves**   loaf loa**ves**   (hoof can be either hoof**s** OR hoo**ves**)
Note: knife kni**ves**   life li**ves**
Some nouns do not add -**s** -**es** -**ies** or -**ves**. Instead they change other letters:
e.g.   child child**ren** / goose gee**se** / man m**en** / mouse m**ice** / ox ox**en**
Other nouns are always plural with no singular version:- e.g. scissors, shorts.
Finally there are some nouns which are <u>the same</u> in the singular or the plural:-
e.g.   aircraft cannon cod   deer salmon sheep
Note: Always <u>check in a dictionary</u> if you are not sure of the spelling of a noun.

Gender

In languages such as French and Latin, all nouns have **gender**. i.e. They are either **masculine** (male) or **feminine** (female) or **neuter** (neither male or female).
e.g. French nouns have *le* or *la* in front of them to show that they are male or female.
In the English language this form of gender does not usually apply. Instead there are several nouns which have a male and a female version, especially when referring to humans or animals.
e.g.   grandfather - grandmother, sir - madam, waiter - waitress, ram - ewe.

Some nouns can be made into male or female versions by adding a masculine or feminine version in front of the noun.
e.g.   "Car for sale. One <u>lady</u> owner." (owner could be either masculine or feminine).

Some people refer to inanimate objects as if they were male or female.
e.g.   Ships, cars or aeroplanes are often called 'her' or 'she':-
          "May God bless all who sail in <u>her</u>."

VERBS - A **verb** is a word which describes movement or action in a sentence. Verbs are also called 'doing' words as they show what someone or something is doing. Verbs can also describe a state of 'being' such as how a person is feeling or what is happening.

Examples - walk, listen, am, have, like, etc.

The ending of a verb depends on its **TENSE**. Traditionally tense refers to the **time** an action occurs. There are three basic tenses with verbs.

PRESENT TENSE:- He listens/he is listening/he does listen - this is happening **now**.
PAST TENSE:- He listened/he was listening - this happened in the **past**.
FUTURE TENSE:- He will listen/he is going to listen - this will happen in the **future**.

Note: When another verb is placed next to the main verb in a sentence, this is called an **AUXILIARY VERB**. (Sometimes these are known as 'helping verbs' as they help the main verb to form its tense).
e.g.   Mike *is* listening.   *Does* Ian like her?   Sally *has* a new car.

The main auxiliary verbs in English are based on the verbs 'to be', 'to do' and 'to have' as in the examples above. The other auxiliary verbs are called **modal verbs**. These can express the notion of whether a thing will happen or not: -
e.g.   *Should* you be doing that?   Sheila *will* listen.   You *must* obey the order.

Verbs can have a **subject** which is either **singular** (one person or one thing) or **plural** (more than one person or several things).

The singular subjects are: 'I' (first person) **- I** was watching; 'you' (second person) - **You** played; 'he'/'she'/'it' (third person) - **He** listens; OR a general thing - **The tree** fell down.

The plural subjects are: 'we' (first person) **- We** were tired; 'you' (second person) - All of **you** can try; 'they' (third person) - **They** are naughty;   OR several things - **The waves** moved quickly.

Note: If the subject is singular, the verb should also be singular and if the subject is plural, then the verb should also be plural.
e.g.   I love, you love, he/she/it loves - singular   We love, you love, they love - plural
Note: For the third person (singular) the verb ends in **-s**. If a verb ends in **ch** or **sh** we add **es** to the verb in this person.
e.g.   I say - he say**s**   You catch - he catch**es**   I wash - she wash**es**

3

The **INFINITIVE** of a verb is when no other endings are added to the verb base. The word 'to' is usually placed in front of it. e.g. Robert had *to listen*. I want *to stay* there.

Note: A "split infinitive" is where an extra word is placed between 'to' and the verb.
e.g.   We had to *quickly* move out of the classroom as a fire had started.

        A better way of saying the above sentence would be:-

        We had to move *quickly* out of the classroom . . . OR
        We had to move out of the classroom *quickly* . . .

PARTICIPLES are where different endings are added to the verb base.

When -**ing** is added to the end of a verb, this is called the **present participle**. It can be used in conjunction with an auxiliary verb.
e.g.   I am listen**ing**   You were try**ing**
The present participle can also be used as a noun. This is called "a **gerund**" or verbal noun.   e.g.   The <u>howling</u> of the wolves woke the villagers.

Note: Words ending in -**ing** can also be used as an adjective.
e.g.   The *running* race.

When -**ed** is added to the end of a verb this is called the **past participle**.
e.g.   He had listen**ed**.   I have stay**ed**.

However, there are many verbs which are **irregular**, which means that they do not follow this rule for the past participle. e.g. known,   seen,   worn. These irregular verbs usually end in:- -**d** -**en** -**n** (e.g. tro**d** beat**en** seen) and will have the one of these words in front of it - had, has, have, was or were.

e.g. John <u>had been</u> home. Or: The netball team <u>was beaten</u> by the opposition

Note: Some endings of verbs will change their spelling when -**ing** or -ed are added:-

e.g.   Change becomes chang**ing**   (the **e** is removed)

The **imperative** is where the verb is used to show commands, requests or prohibitions:-

e.g.   command - *Sit* down now! request - Please *go* to bed!
        prohibition - Don't *speak* to me like that!

Verbs can also be either **active** or **passive**. This means that the subject verb is either doing something (active), or having something done to it (passive).

e.g.   The man opened the door - active
         The door was opened by the man - passive

Connected with active and passive verbs is the notion of **voice**. This is how a writer uses active or passive verbs in a sentence to get across to the reader what is happening in a sentence.

e.g.   I sang the carol - active voice
         The carol was sung by me - passive voice

In the first example (active voice), the subject is **I** who sings the carol. In the second example (passive voice), the subject is **the carol** which is sung by me.

Verbs can also be **transitive** or **intransitive**. A transitive verb is one that needs to have an object in the sentence with it, otherwise the sentence would not make sense.

e.g.   The cook made . . .

The verb 'made' is transitive as it needs an object to complete the sentence. Thus the sentence would be complete with:-

         The cook made a meat pie.

An intransitive verb is one that doesn't need an object in the sentence.

e.g.   The bird flies.   The pet died.

Note: Some verbs can be used as transitive verbs or as intransitive verbs:

e.g.   The fire burnt his hand. (transitive)   The fire burnt quickly. (intransitive)

Verbs which have a subject are called **finite** verbs. e.g. She **ate** an apple.

Non-finite parts of verbs do not have a subject. There are three types of these:-

1)   The present participle   e.g. **Working** late, meant he would miss the match.

2)   The past participle   e.g. "**Gone** already?" enquired the lady at the station.

3)   The infinitive   e.g. He wants **to go** now and not in ten minutes.

PRONOUNS - A **pronoun** is a word which is used in the place of a noun in a sentence and is usually a short word:-
Examples - I, he, she, it, we, they, you, him, her, they, us, yours, my, mine, those, whose, theirs, ours, that.

As with nouns, there are several different types of pronouns which have particular functions: -

PERSONAL PRONOUNS
Examples - I, we, he, she, they, you, us, it.

They are usually used in the place of a proper noun and are often the subject of a sentence.

e.g.   Instead of writing: Mr. Hayes paid the money out
              you write: *He* paid the money out.

Or they can be used by themselves:- *You* liked the book.

RELATIVE PRONOUNS
Examples - that, which, what, who.

Relative pronouns always join together two sentences or phrases.

e.g.   This is the key *that* opens the door.

POSSESSIVE PRONOUNS
Examples - his, hers, theirs, ours, my, mine.

Possessive pronouns show who owns or possesses something.

e.g.   That boat is *his* .   This car is *mine*.

REFLEXIVE PRONOUNS
Examples - herself, himself, itself, myself, ourselves, yourself, yourselves.

Reflexive pronouns are used where the subject and object are one and the same people.

e.g.   They hurt *themselves* badly in the accident.

Note: Reflexive pronouns are sometimes called **compound pronouns**.

DEMONSTRATIVE PRONOUNS
Examples - that, this, these, those.

Demonstrative pronouns indicate or demonstrate things or people..

e.g.   *That* is the wrong question. *These* are the culprits.

INTERROGATIVE PRONOUNS
Examples - who? when? what? why? which? whose? whom?

Interrogative pronouns are used to ask a question.

e.g.   *Whose* is that car? *When* is the bus going to arrive?

Note: There are also interrogative adjectives which are the same words. They differ from interrogative pronouns in that a noun always follows them.

e.g.   *Whose* <u>car</u> is that ? *What* <u>bus</u> is going to arrive ?

INDEFINITE PRONOUNS
Examples - all, anybody, anyone, both, each, everybody, nobody, one.

Indefinite pronouns refer to all other pronouns which do not have a 'definite' purpose yet are still pronouns.

e.g.   "*Nobody* move!" shouted the bank robber.
        "*Anybody* in?" asked the policeman.

DETERMINERS - A **determiner** is a word which is used to determine or show the limit of a noun in different ways.

e.g.   <u>the</u> dog,   <u>our</u> friends,   <u>ten</u> detached houses, etc.

Note: The noun always comes after the determiner, but not always immediately.

Most determiners are words which are frequently used in English. They can be articles (<u>a</u> man), demonstratives (<u>that</u> boy), possessives (<u>your</u> car), numbers (<u>twenty</u> geese), quantifiers (a <u>few</u> coins), or question words (<u>which</u> way?).

Determiners can also be used as pronouns where a noun has been replaced by the pronoun.

e.g.   <u>That</u> is mine (where 'that' could be referring to 'that coat')

ADJECTIVES - An **adjective** is a word that is used to describe a noun or a pronoun, such as what sort of noun it is, or how much there is of it.

Examples - blue, strong, most, large, two, last.

e.g.   A *little* girl.   The *broken* window.   *Three* cats.

Note: Most adjectives come before the noun, though they can come after it as well.

e.g.   The boat, *tiny* by our standards.   Helen was *pretty*.

Note: In the second example the adjective comes after the verb (*was*) but is still describing the noun (*Helen*).

Adjectives can be divided into several different groups:

QUALITY ADJECTIVES   These are adjectives which tell us something about the noun.
i.e. what 'qualities' it has, such as "What colour is it?"   "How big is it?" etc.

e.g.   A *brown* bag.   A *massive* building.

QUANTITY ADJECTIVES   These are used to tell us the amount or quantity of a noun. Examples: one, two, third, many, a few, etc.
(This group includes 'number adjectives')

e.g.   The *fifth* girl fell over.   *Most* of the seagulls flew away.

DEMONSTRATIVE ADJECTIVES   These are used to distinguish one noun from another noun.   Examples: these, those, this etc.

e.g.   *That* lady is older than the other one.

POSSESSIVE ADJECTIVES These adjectives show who owns or possesses something.   Examples: my, mine, yours, its, etc.

e.g.   It was *our* school that won the championship.

INTERROGATIVE ADJECTIVES   These are adjectives that are used in questions.   Examples: what, which, whose, etc.

e.g.   *What* date will it be a week on Tuesday ?

COMPARISON OF ADJECTIVES

Adjectives can be compared to each other by adding the suffixes, -er and -est to the ends of the adjectives.

e.g.   small (**nominative**)   smaller (**comparative)**   smallest (**superlative**)

This works with most adjectives if they have just one or two syllables. However there are some adjectives with two or three syllables where this pattern does not work. Instead, the words 'more' and 'most' are put in front of the adjective.

e.g.   difficult (nominative) more   difficult   (comparative)   most   difficult (superlative)

Note: The nominative category of adjective is also known as the **Positive**.

ADVERBS - An **adverb** is a word that is used to describe what a verb is doing in a sentence. Examples - quickly, fast, hard, furiously.
There are four main categories of adverb. In each category, the adverb can answer different questions that are asked about the verb.

1) **ADVERBS OF MANNER** They answer the question **how?**
e.g.   The boy answered the question *easily*.

2) **ADVERBS OF PLACE** They answer the question **where ?**
e.g.   The burglar was hiding *upstairs* in the house.

3) **ADVERBS OF TIME** They answer the question **when ?**
e.g.   The washing machine repair took *all day*.

4) **ADVERBS OF DEGREE** They answer the questions **how much** or **how often?**
e.g.   He ran around the block *twice* before breakfast.

Note: Most (but not all) adverbs end in 'ly'.
e.g.   The old lady fell *badly*.   Note: He thought *hard*.

Sentence adverbs link parts of a sentence together.
Examples: rather, so, therefore

e.g.   He would *rather* stay at home than go to the football match.

Note: Some adverbs can also be adjectives depending on the context:

e.g.   He was a *friendly* man (adjective) She was very *friendly* (adverb)

PREPOSITIONS - A **preposition** is a word which tells us what the relationship is between two nouns (or pronouns) in a sentence. It comes after the first noun (or pronoun) and goes in front of the second noun in a sentence.

e.g.   The cat lay *beside* the dog.   We pushed our way *inside* the building.

Examples - about, above, across, after, against, along, among, at, beside, between, beyond, by, down, for, in, inside, into, near, of, off, on, over, since, through, to, towards, under, underneath, until, up, upon, with.

Note: Prepositions can be used together in a sentence: -

e.g.   He came from *down under.*

Propositions can show such things as position, time, direction, possession, etc.

e.g.   The school was *next to* the Police station. He came *during* the day.

Note: There are several prepositions that can be formed by two or three words.

e.g.   as far as, because of, except for, in spite of, on to, with regard to.

(This type of preposition is sometimes called a **compound preposition**).

CONJUNCTIONS - A **conjunction** is a word which joins together words, phrases or clauses within a sentence.   (see also connectives on page 24)

Examples -   although, and, but, for, or, so, etc.

e.g.   Over *and* out. (joining words)   At nine *or* at ten. (joining phrases)
        He tried hard, *but* he could not finish the test. (joining clauses)

Note: There are some conjunctions that occur in pairs in sentences. Usually these are written to show two different ideas or opinions:

Examples -   Either...or / not only... but / neither...nor / so ... as

e.g.   You will finish your homework *whether* you like it *or* not.

Some conjunctions help to show the notion of time, place, degree or purpose. Examples -   after, as, since, so that, when, where, while, etc.

e.g.   Make sure you brush your teeth *before* you go to bed.

INTERJECTIONS - An **interjection** is a word that shows an **exclamation** in a word or sentence. All sorts of strong feelings can be shown in an interjection such as:

> pleasure - *Fantastic ! Marvellous !*
> shock or surprise - *Wow ! Oh !*
> hatred - *Fool ! Stupid !*

Words that are used in **greetings** are also interjections.

e.g.   Hello ! Good morning !

Orders too can be interjections.   e.g.   Attention !   Sit down !

Note: All interjections/exclamations are followed by exclamation marks !!!

ARTICLES   These are the three different words that can come in front of nouns and adjectives. They are a type of determiner.

The **definite article** is the word "**the**".

This is put in front of a noun or an adjective in a sentence.

e.g.   The field (noun)   The glittering ...... (adjective)

Note: "The" is pronounced "thu" in front of words that begin with a consonant sound and pronounced "thee" in front of words that begin with a vowel sound.

The **indefinite articles** are the words "**a**" and "**an**". These are put in front of singular nouns to show that there is only one of something.

e.g.   A man,   an elephant.

'a' goes in front of words that begin with a consonant sound:- a car, a tree, etc.
'an' goes in front of words that begin with a vowel sound:- an octopus, an arch, etc.

Note: The indefinite article, 'an' is used in front of some words that begin with the letter 'h' if it is pronounced without the h sound. E.g. An hour, an heir. Some words that begin with the letter 'h' and which are pronounced with the 'h' sound sometimes have 'an' put in front of them like 'an hotel', but this is not as common as in the past.

PUNCTUATION

PUNCTUATION MARKS are used in sentences to point out when a sentence ends, what it is saying and what its meaning is. Without punctuation marks any piece of writing would be very difficult to read, as well as to say out loud. Punctuation marks help the reader or speaker know when to pause, when to take a breath or when to emphasise a certain word or phrase. For example, without full stops, question marks and exclamation marks, you wouldn't know when it is the end of the sentence.

This first group of punctuation marks all belong to the "**long stops**" group of punctuation marks, meaning that they are used to end a sentence. These are full stops, question marks and exclamation marks.

FULL STOPS (.) Full stops always come at the end of a sentence to show that it has finished. The next letter following a full stop should always be a capital letter.

e.g.   Stuart decided to stop running. He felt much better.

The end of the first sentence is straight after the word "running". Note the next word - "He" - has a capital letter, as it is the start of the next sentence.

Note: Full stops are not always used to indicate the end of a sentence. A question mark or an exclamation mark are sometimes used. (see below)

Full stops are also used to show an abbreviation:-

e.g.   p.m. or A.D. or   Mr H. Smith.

With the first two examples, full stops have been included, though this practice is not always used nowadays. With the third example, full stops are still put after the initials of a person's name. Words which have had letters removed, particularly from the last few letters: e.g.   approx (from approximately) or Mr (From Mister) do not have to have a full stop after them.

Full stops can also be used:-

in money: e.g.   £3.50
in decimal numbers (as in the decimal point):   e.g.   35.45
in times:-   e.g.   2.15. pm or 16.37.

Note: In American English the full stop is called 'a period'.

QUESTION MARKS (?) Question marks also come at the end of a sentence, to show that a question is being asked.

e.g.   Where is the railway station ?

When a question is written as a quotation, the question mark is put inside the quotation marks:-

"Where is the railway station?" I enquired.

Note: Sometimes single words can have a question mark put after them if they are "question words".

e.g.   How ?   Where ?   Why ?   etc.

EXCLAMATION MARKS (!) Exclamation marks come at the end of a sentence when an **interjection** is used. This is a word which shows the feelings of pleasure, surprise or shock.

e.g.   That was disgusting !   The show was fantastic !   Aaahh !

Exclamation marks can also be put at the end of phrases or sentences when you want to emphasise something funny, or if a command or order is being issued.

e.g.   Sit down !   Be quiet !   He got covered in custard !!!

Note: Some writers use two or more exclamation marks to exaggerate the humour in a sentence.

This second group of punctuation marks all belong to the "**short stops**" group of punctuation marks, which are used inside a sentence to help break it up into smaller sections. These are:- commas, semi-colons, colons, hyphens, dashes and brackets.

COMMAS (,) Commas have several different functions, most of which are concerned with separating words, clauses or phrases within sentences.

Commas are used to break up a sentence into smaller sections so that it makes sense. In the sentence below, commas separate three of the four sections.

e.g.   I went for a walk in the forest, looked at the trees, crossed the stream and then I came home.

Commas are used when there is a list of things which need to be separated. This could be a list of nouns (first example) or a list of adjectives (second example).

e.g. For breakfast he had bacon, eggs, sausages, toast, jam and tea.

His speech was challenging, rousing, disturbing and thought provoking.

Note: In the first example there is no comma after jam, but instead the last word in the list, tea, is preceded by 'and' rather than a comma. This is the usual practice in English, though in American English a comma would be put in just before the "and".

Commas are used in instructions to separate the different parts of the instruction.

e.g. Put in an egg, mix with flour, add some water and bake for twenty minutes.

Commas are used to end direct speech within a sentence.

e.g. "You may have some more sweets," said Mum.

Note: If there is a question mark or an exclamation mark after the direct speech, a comma is not used.

Commas are used to separate a person from the rest of the sentence.

e.g. "Sally, please don't do that!" said the teacher.

Commas are used to separate parts of a sentence which are not necessary to the rest of the sentence.

e.g. Michael, the head boy, read the lesson in assembly.

In the above example you could have said either "the head boy read the lesson" or "Michael read the lesson". So, either the name of the boy, 'Michael', or his position, 'Head Boy', are not needed to make the sentence make sense. This is called being in **apposition** to each other.

Commas are used to mark off sentence adverbs from the rest of the sentence.

e.g. My thoughts, therefore, are that this is not a good idea.

Commas are used to separate the words **who(m)** or **which** from the rest of the sentence.

e.g. The horse, which had fallen badly, had to be put down.

SEMI-COLON (;) Semi-colons are used to separate two clauses or groups of words within a sentence. (These two clauses could also be separate sentences which are connected to each other by their subject matter). Semi-colons can be used instead of conjunctions such as "and" or "but".

e.g.   The lady dropped her handbag; all the contents fell out. ('and' could have been used instead of the semi-colon).

Semi-colons can also be used to separate different items in a long list, where each item is made up of several words.

e.g.   The new car has these features: a choice of striking colours; four-door central locking; air-bags for the driver and passengers; engine immobiliser and alarm; side-impact safety bars; and air-conditioning.

COLON (:) Colons are used just before there is a list of things in a sentence or before a quotation.

e.g.   People had come from all over the country: from Derby, from Newcastle,   from Birmingham and from Liverpool.

e.g.   The inscription read: "He lived his life to the full".

Note: Sometimes a dash can be added to the colon, especially if it follows the words 'as follows'.

e.g.   The programme for the day will be as follows:- breakfast, lecture, coffee . .

Colons are also used in numbers, such as when a Bible verse is used - John 4:20, or in times - 14:53. (This is mainly in American English as Standard English uses a full stop between numbers - 14.53).

BRACKETS ( ) Brackets are used to enclose an extra thought or piece of information which is not the main part of a sentence. They are sometimes called **'parentheses'** (as in American English) and are always used in pairs.

e.g.   The UFO (Unidentified Flying Object) was seen by several witnesses.

or   Mr. Jones (who used to deliver the papers) has moved away.

Brackets can also be used to enclose page numbers or dates.

e.g.   Elizabeth I (1558 - 1603) was the last Tudor monarch.

HYPHEN (-) Hyphens are usually used to join two or more words together to make compound words, including town names.

e.g.   Heart-ache, fall-out.   Newcastle-upon-Tyne, Leigh-on-Sea.

Note: Nowadays, most compound words tend not to use hyphens at all. The main exceptions are: **compound nouns** where the second part is a short word:-
e.g.   a lift-up, a sell-off, a tie-in   OR **compound adjectives** which are used as modifiers before the noun. e.g. a part-time worker,   an eight-year-old boy.

Hyphens are also used in words where there are two letters the same next to each other, such as 'ee' or 'oo', in order to separate them.
e.g.   co-ordinates, re-examine.

Finally, hyphens can sometimes be used at the end of a line to show that a broken word continues on the next line.
e.g.   He fell over whilst walking in the for-
        est one day.

Note: Words which are cut off at the end of a line should be broken up into their syllables (hard - ly) and not between syllables (ha - rdly). If the word has only one syllable (i.e. a **monosyllabic** word), you should not hyphenate this word at all.

DASHES (—) Dashes are longer than hyphens and can be used in the place of brackets to show a different idea from the rest of the sentence.

e.g.   We travelled across the Irish Sea — minus our luggage — on a fast ship.

Dashes can also be used to separate words that are repeated next to each other.

e.g.   He forgot the map — the map which would show him the way to go.

Dashes can also be used in the place of commas to cut off words in apposition.

e.g.   They were a first-rate team — unbeaten in twenty matches — who would go down in history.

Dashes can also be used to show a change of opinion or direction.

e.g.   You must turn left after the traffic lights — no turn right, then go on for about a mile — or is it half a mile ?

Remember: Dashes go between parts of a sentence, whilst hyphens go between parts of a word. A dash is longer than a hyphen. A hyphen is shorter than a dash.

INVERTED COMMAS (' ') **or** (" ") Inverted Commas are pairs of commas which have been inverted (i.e. turned upside down) to show the words spoken in written English. They are sometimes called **Quotation Marks** or **Speech Marks**. They are mainly used in pairs, though increasingly they are used as single inverted commas.

e.g.   "How are you today?" asked the old man.

or   'I liked your picture,' said Sam's teacher.

Note: Other punctuation marks such as commas, question marks and exclamation marks all come <u>inside</u> the second pair of inverted commas.

Sometimes the same spoken words are divided up into two parts by words such as **said** or something similar. In cases like this, inverted commas must be put around both sets of spoken words.

e.g.   "Mary is wrong," shouted John, "because she picked the wrong answer."

Inverted commas are not just used to show what words are being spoken but are also used to show titles of a book, film, song, television programme or play, etc.

e.g.   'The Wind In The Willows'.   'Blue Peter'.

Note: when using inverted commas within direct speech it is common practice to use single inverted commas next to double inverted commas.

e.g.   "I really liked 'Star Wars'," said Sophie.

Note: a comma is used to separate the different inverted commas. However, if you are writing a title of something on a word processor it is better to use *italics* rather than speech marks. e.g. 'I really liked *Star Wars*', said Sophie.

Sometimes inverted commas/speech marks are used to show irony.

e.g.   The child feigned 'an illness' so that he could be excused from PE.

DIRECT SPEECH is the name given to the words spoken by a person and should always start and end with inverted commas, whilst **INDIRECT SPEECH** concerns spoken words which are reported by a different person. They do not have inverted commas around them and are not the exact words spoken.

e.g.   Jane said, "I would like some ice cream." (direct speech)

         Jane said that she would like some ice cream. (indirect speech)

Remember: When changing from direct to indirect speech, the writer will usually have to change some or all of the following parts of the sentence:

1)   Personal pronouns - e.g. 'you' becomes 'we'
2)   Verb tenses. e.g. - 'are' becomes 'were'
3)   Adverbs to do with place and time - e.g. 'today' becomes 'yesterday'
4)   Possessive adjectives - e.g. 'your' becomes 'our'

e.g.   The tourists asked us, "Do you know if there are there any good films on at your cinema today?"

When the sentence above, which is written in direct speech, is changed to indirect speech, the new sentence reads: -

The tourists asked us if we knew whether there were any good films on at our cinema today.

Remember when changing from direct to indirect speech to add the words 'that' or 'if' or 'whether' or 'to', if necessary.

Note: **Reported speech** is another name for indirect speech.

ELLIPSIS (. . .) These three dots are used to show that something is incomplete in a sentence or that something has been missed out of a sentence. These dots are sometimes called an **ellipsis** and can also show a break in a sentence.

e.g.   We really didn't know . . . . what would happen next.

They can also be used to end a sentence where the ending is unclear.

e.g.   That was the last of him. Or so we thought . . .

ASTERISK (*) This punctuation mark is used by some writers in various ways.

It can be used to replace letters in swear words or taboo words so that the actual word cannot be fully seen. e.g. Bl***y.

It can be used to show a footnote at the end of the piece of writing, or it can be used to show important parts of a text.

APOSTROPHES (') Apostrophes are like commas which have been lifted up from the line on a page. They are used to show that a letter or letters have been removed from a word. Usually they are placed inside two words which have been shortened to form one longer word.

e.g.   **Is not** becomes **isn't** when the 'o' is removed and an apostrophe is put in   its place. The two words are then squeezed together.

Words like this that have been shortened by the insertion of an apostrophe are called **contractions**. The most common ones can be seen on page 40.

Apostrophes are also used to show **possession**. i.e. that something belongs to someone else.

e.g.   Michael's car. This the short way of saying "The car belonging to Michael."

There are certain rules when using the apostrophe in cases like this.

Firstly, if the word is singular and does not end in **s**, you use an apostrophe followed by **s**.

e.g.   Cheryl's house (the house belonging to Cheryl).

Secondly, if the word is singular and ends in an **s** the apostrophe is added after that **s** and then another **s** is added.

e.g.   Jesus' s teaching. (The teaching of Jesus).

Thirdly, if the word is plural ending in **s** or **es**, you add an apostrophe after the **s**.

e.g.   The clowns' clothes. (The clothes belonging to the clowns).
         The foxes' lair. (The lair belonging to the foxes).

Fourthly, if the word is plural but doesn't end in **s**, you add the apostrophe and then the **s**.

e.g.   The women's changing room. (The changing room belonging to the women).

Note: Some words that end in s don't have an apostrophe added to them at all. The most common one is 'its' which should not be confused with "it's" which is short for "it is". The other words ending in s which don't add an apostrophe include: hers   his   ours   theirs   and   yours.   These are all **possessive pronouns**.

CAPITAL LETTERS (A B C etc.) Capital letters are always used in the first letter of the first word that is used at the beginning of a sentence. If there is a full stop, the next letter should be a capital letter.

e.g.   Peter bought an ice cream at the shop. He paid £1.20 for it.

Capital letters are also used as the first letter of names of people, places and things.

e.g.   Simon, Sarah Jones, Brazil, England, the Times, High Street, the Grand Hotel, Oxford University, the River Thames. etc.

Capital letters are also used to begin adjectives which are based on proper nouns.

e.g.   Japanese, Elizabethan, Mancunian, African, etc.

Capital letters are also used for the main words in the titles of songs, films, books and plays.

e.g.   "Bohemian Rhapsody". "The Wizard of Oz". "The Koran".

The letter 'i' by itself is written as a capital letter, 'I' in written English, as are most initials when used as abbreviations, such as 'BBC'.

e.g.   I thought that I had said the correct thing.

Capital letters are also used for the days of the week and for months of the year.

e.g.   Today is Tuesday 21st March 2000.

Note: The seasons - spring, summer, autumn, winter - do not have capital letters.

Capital letters are used in official titles such as: "The Archbishop of Canterbury" and "Sir Robert Peel".

Capital letters are also used in the word "God" as well as the pronouns associated with God:-

E.g.   the Lord, He, Him, etc.

Finally, capital letters are used when it is the first word of direct speech as well as to begin each line in poetry:-

e.g.   'Hello, Mrs. Wright,' he said.

GRAMMAR

The English language is made up of words arranged in different ways. The way English is written and spoken is dependant on many different rules and customs. The basic collection of words is called a **sentence**.

SENTENCES A sentence starts with a capital letter and ends with a full stop, (or a question mark or an exclamation mark). Sentences can be one of several types.

Firstly, a sentence can be a **statement** or a **thought** from one person to another.

e.g.   "I enjoyed the film". This is called a **declarative sentence** as it declares or announces something.

Secondly, a sentence can be an **order** or **command**.

e.g.   " Stop doing that!" This is called an **imperative sentence** as it is giving out an instruction or a command.

Thirdly, a sentence can be a **request** or a **question**.

e.g.   "How did you do that?" This is called an **interrogative sentence** as it is asking a question.

Fourthly, a sentence can be an **exclamation**.

e.g.   "That was weird!" This is called an **exclamative sentence** as it is showing surprise or emotion.

Syntax is the word used to describe how a sentence is constructed. Below are the main things needed to make a good sentence.

A sentence usually contains a subject and a predicate .

The **subject** of a sentence is the main part of a sentence and tells the reader who or what is doing something. This is always a noun. The **predicate** forms the rest of the sentence and tells the reader about what the subject did. This contains a verb and a noun at least.

e.g.   The teacher spoke to the children.

In the above example, "The teacher" (a noun), is the subject and "spoke to the children" (a verb, a preposition and a noun), is the predicate.

Adding either a clause or a phrase can extend sentences. A **clause** is a group of words in a sentence (including a verb) which can do the work of a noun, adjective or an adverb.

e.g.   The teacher spoke to the children **because he was angry with them.**

This clause explains why the teacher spoke to the children and is doing the job of an adjective as it describes what sort of teacher he was. It could just as easily have been written as: 'The angry teacher spoke to the children'.

Clauses can be either **main clauses** which make up the main part of a sentence, or **subordinate clauses** which give extra information to a main clause which is already in a sentence.

A **phrase** is a collection of words which make up part of a sentence. Phrases usually have two or more words in them and don't make sense on their own and <u>don't</u> contain a verb.

e.g.   The teacher spoke to the children **in the classroom.**

There are several types of phrases. Here are the five types of phrase with examples:-

Noun phrase - **a good girl**
Verb phrase - they **talked loudly**
Adverbial phrase - She rushed **all the way home**
Adjectival phrase - The dog **with the very loud bark**
Prepositional phrase - The book is **on the shelf** (this connects the two nouns)

Apart from having a subject, a sentence also has an **object**. This is usually the second noun in a sentence and explains what the verb does in the sentence.

e.g.   She carried <u>the doll</u>.   'the doll' is the object here.

The object of a sentence is sometimes called the **direct object** if it is the only object in a sentence as in the above example. If the action of the verb affects something *indirectly* in a sentence, the object is then called the **indirect object**.

e.g.   He threw the ball to Sam.

Here 'Sam' is the indirect object as there is already an object in the sentence - 'the ball', which is the direct object.

Sentences can be one of three types: - <u>simple</u> , <u>compound</u> or <u>complex</u> .

Simple sentences

A simple sentence is one which has only one verb and which describes only one thing.

e.g.   I like to watch the television.

Compound sentences

A compound sentence is one which is made up of two or more simple sentences (or clauses) which are joined by conjunctions such as 'and', 'by', 'with' etc.

e.g.   He was running to the bus stop **so** that he would not miss the bus.

Complex sentences

A complex sentence is one which contains a main clause as well as a subordinate clause. It usually contains all the parts necessary to make up a complete sentence:- noun, verb, pronoun, adjective, adverb, determiner, preposition, conjunction, articles and interjection. It can also have more than one verb and describe more than one thing.

e.g.   "Take care!" warned the wise old man to the group of students who were
         listening to everything he said.

Here are some other terms associated with sentences and sentence construction, which are relevant to primary aged children.

Agreement

This refers to the subject and the verb in a sentence that must agree in number, gender or case otherwise the sentence would be grammatically incorrect.

e.g.   'He have....' is wrong. It should be 'He has'.   'Tomorrow I was sad' should be 'Tomorrow I will be sad'.

(The term **concord** is a formal word that also means agreement).

Complement

This refers to verbs in sentences which by themselves would be incomplete:

e.g.   She was . . .   It is . . .   Steven is . . .

Thus the words that are added to these incomplete verbs are called 'the complement'.   e.g. She was *beautiful*   It is *raining*   Steven   is   *good   at chess*.

Conditional

This is a sentence which says that one thing is dependant upon another thing. These sentences often begin with conjunctions such as 'if', 'provided', 'unless', 'as long as', etc.

e.g.   If you carry on like that, you will have an accident.

This means that if you do one thing, something will happen as a result. Conditionals also refer to   verb forms such as: 'will', 'may', 'would' and 'should'.

Connectives

A connective is a word or phrase that is used to connect clauses or sentences together. Connectives can be either conjunctions (and, but) or connecting adverbs (therefore, for example).

e.g.   We enjoyed going to the cinema *because* it was an interesting film.

The word "because" is the connective here as it joins the two parts of the sentence to make one long sentence.

Here is a list of some of the main connectives:-

after / although / and /   as / as long as / as soon as / because / before / but / despite / except / however / in spite of / nevertheless / otherwise / rather than / since /   so   that / sooner   than /   therefore / unless / whereas / while

Embedding

This is where a clause is put inside a sentence rather than adding it to the end with a conjunction.

e.g.   The fireman put out the fire *by* spraying the extinguisher   becomes:
        The fireman, spraying the extinguisher, put out the fire.

Idiom

This is an expression which is not meant to be taken literally, but whose meaning is understood by those who speak or write it. They are sometimes called **idiomatic expressions**. **Colloquialisms** would also fit into this category.

e.g.   'He's lost his marbles' means   'he's not in his right mind'.
        'She'd lost the plot'   means   'she didn't understand'.
        'He was in a right two and eight'   means 'he was in a state . . of worry'.

Whilst these are part of everyday spoken English they should not be used in written English, unless they are being used as a quotation from a certain character.

Inversion
This is where the verb comes before the subject noun in a sentence. Instead of saying, "Such a case rarely baffled him", with inversion we would say, "Rarely had such a case baffled him". In the second sentence, the auxiliary verb, 'had', comes before the subject noun, 'a case'. This is the inversion or "reversal" of the verb and subject noun.

Tautology
This is the use of extra words in a phrase or a sentence to emphasise an idea when a single word would fit just as well.

e.g.   The <u>ancient</u> <u>old</u> man is a <u>modest</u> <u>humble</u> person.

Usage
This is where a word or phrase is used in written or spoken English that is not grammatically correct, but which is commonly accepted by the majority of people in a certain situation. **Slang** words are examples of usage. A **cliché** is another term connected with usage, where a word becomes a cliché because it is over-used by many people and loses its original sense. e.g. wicked absolutely.

Figures of Speech

Figures of Speech are certain tools, which writers use to give their writing extra strength and make it more powerful or colourful. It is sometimes called "**figurative language**" and is language that is not to be taken literally. The main figures of speech are discussed below.

Metaphor A metaphor is when a writer speaks about something as if it were something else which it might be similar to.

e.g.   Mr. Jones, the old dog, was very cruel to the child.

Here Mr. Jones is likened to an old dog as a way of showing that his actions were more like those of a dog than of a human.

Connected with a metaphor is **personification** where language that is connected to human emotions or actions is used to refer to inanimate ideas or objects.

e.g.   The gods were playing a little joke on him.   OR   Hope never fails.

Epigram This is a slightly funny saying, which gives the effect of making it sound humorous.

e.g.   His hair style was like nothing on earth !

Simile A simile is when one thing is compared to something else in writing, even though it may be slightly different in reality. A simile can be spotted by the use of the words: "as . . . as a . . .". They can compare something or someone with either the qualities of animals/creatures or objects/things.

e.g.   Andrew was as blind as a bat. (a simile showing an animal quality) This sentence means that Andrew cannot see very well and is not literally blind.

Or   The child looked as white as a sheet. (a simile showing a quality of a thing) This sentence means that the child was very pale and not literally white.

Some well known animal quality similes:-

As busy as a bee
As fat as a pig
As happy as a lark
As hungry as a wolf
As playful as a kitten
As proud as a peacock
As quiet as a mouse
As strong as an ox
As wise as an owl

Some well known object similes:

As black as coal
As bold as brass
As clear as crystal
As cold as ice
As flat as a pancake
As green as grass
As quick as lightning
As right as rain
As ugly as sin

Alliteration This refers to the process of using the same phoneme or initial letters of several words together in a sentence or line of poetry.

e.g.   Heather had hated her husband for many years.

Here the letter 'H' is used in the first five words of the sentence.

Euphemism This is when a word or words are used to "cover up" the real meaning of a word so that it will not offend someone or hurt their feelings.

e.g.   "To spend a penny" is a euphemism for going to the toilet.
"She passed away" is a euphemism for saying that she has died.

Onomatopoeia This is the use of certain words which make a sound similar to or connected with the word being used.

e.g.   The snake hissed at the tiger.

Rhetorical Question This is a question that is being asked that doesn't need someone to answer it, as the answer is obvious.

e.g.   "Why can't you behave?" is really saying
"You should behave better than you are doing".

SPELLING

Words are made up of **letters**, which are arranged in different ways. The way the letters are arranged is called its **spelling**. There are 26 different letters in the English **alphabet** which are based on the Roman alphabet:-

a b c d e f g h i j k l m n o p q r s t u v w x y z (lower case letters)

A B C D E F G H I J K L M N O P Q R S T U V W X Y Z
(upper case letters - also known as capital letters)

"The quick brown fox jumped over the lazy cows" is a famous sentence, which incorporates every one of the 26 letters of the English alphabet, except for 'g'. (The word 'alphabet' actually comes from the first two letters of the Greek alphabet - alpha and beta). When letters are arranged in **alphabetical order** it means they are arranged in the same order as in the alphabet - 'a' comes before 'b', 'r' comes before 's' etc. If several words begin with the same letter, in order to put them in alphabetical order, you have to look at the second letter, or even the third letter of the word and so on.

e.g.   after, accident, almost, accent, adder, almighty
         put in alphabetical order would be:
         accent, accident, adder, after, almighty, almost
         with acce coming before acci, ad, af, almi and almo.

Ascenders are the parts of letters, which ascend or go higher than the main letter shape. Thus b, d, f, h, i, k, l and t all have ascenders. **Descenders** are the parts of letters, which hang below the line. Thus g, j, p, q, y (and sometimes f) all have descenders. The remaining letters - a, c, e, m, n, o, r, s, u, v, w, x, z - have the same height

Vowels are sounds which can be represented by the vowel letters: **a e i o u**. Vowels are formed by the sound of your breath coming out of your mouth without any interference from your tongue, teeth or lips. Every word in the English language contains vowels though not all of them have the vowel letters in them. e.g. 'rhythm' or 'hymn' do not have a e i o or u in them. Instead these words have a letter 'y' in them which gives the word a vowel sound. The main vowel sounds are listed on the next page.

Consonants are speech sounds which can be represented by the consonant letters: **b c d f g h j k l m n p q r s t v w x y z**. Consonants are formed by the sound of your breath coming out of your mouth being affected by your lips, tongue or teeth. Nearly every word in the English language has at least one consonant in it.

The smallest unit of sound that you get in a word is called a **phoneme**. One, two, three or even four letters can represent this sound.

e.g.   the 'o' sound as in go oh owe dough .

A **digraph** is where you get two letters representing one phoneme.

e.g.   pain smash lead,

A **trigraph** is where you get three letters representing one phoneme.

e.g.   judge sigh .

A **diphthong** refers to the sound created by two vowel sounds said together, such as 'o' and 'i' as in the word 'joint'.

Other diphthongs include: **i** - as in nice, **ow** - as in owl and **u** - as in cube.

There are twenty vowel phonemes in the English language. Twelve of them are pure vowel phonemes and eight of them are diphthongs. They can either be short vowel sounds or long vowel sounds. Here are some examples:

'a'	-	ant, cat (short)	ace, pay (long)
'e'	-	den, send (short)	ease, week (long)
'i'	-	sing, sit (short)	lie, fright (long)
'o'	-	lot, clog (short)	snow, goal (long)
'u'	-	gun, must (short)	cruel, united (long)

The letter 'y' also has short and long vowel sounds when used as a vowel in words:-

'y'   -   hymn, symbol (short)   spy, lyre (long) as in the letter 'i'

happy, partly (long) as in the letter 'e'

There are also (approximately) twenty-four consonant phonemes in the English language, (depending on a person's **accent**).

Apart from the basic sounds made from vowels, there are several mixtures of vowels and consonants which make different sounds. These are called **blends**. These go mainly at the beginning of words, though some of them are used at the end of words. Here are some of the main blends used in English and the sounds they make:-

bl- as in black   **br**- as in bring   **cl**- as in class   **cr**- as in crate

dr- as in dress   **pl** - as in play   **pr** - as in press   **sl** - as in slot   **st**- as in steal

Assonance is when you get vowel sounds repeated in consecutive words: e.g.   he made eighty pounds,   the owner sold it, etc.

A **grapheme** is where a sound is written down. It can be one or more letters such as a, ar, or, ur, etc.

Syllables are the beats or units in each word, which contain at least one vowel. e.g. hun-dred or miss-ing. Words with only one beat are called **monosyllabic** words. e.g. mask, sound, etc. Words, which have two or more beats, are called **polysyllabic**. e.g. hanger (two syllables), dangerous (three syllables).

A **segment** breaks a word down further into the phonemes that make up the syllables. e.g. hanger would be h-ang-er.

An **onset** is the part of a word that comes in front of a vowel in any syllable.
One, two or three letters can form it. e.g. **str** as in straight.
Note: some words do not have an onset. e.g. only
A **rime** is a part of a syllable, which contains a vowel and a following
consonant (if it has one). e.g. m<u>ate</u> <u>for</u> <u>gel</u>
Some rimes can be complete words in themselves. e.g. an   ice or
A **morpheme** is the smallest unit of meaning there is. This can include
prefixes and suffixes (see below). e.g. build has one morpheme. build/er has
two morphemes, house/build/er has three morphemes, etc.
A **letter string** is when you get several letters together which make a
morpheme or a phoneme; another name for this is **cluster**. e.g. a, r, e, make
'are'.
A **logograph** is a character or symbol that is used to represent a word.
e.g.   & or £ or $.

The majority of words in English do not end in the vowel letters a, i, o or u.
Note: Words that have the vowel sound of 'ee', end in a 'y' - daily, friendly,
etc. Words that do end in these five vowel letters are usually foreign words,
which have been incorporated into the English language: e.g. drama, polo.

Some other spelling terms

Acronym   - An acronym is a word formed from the initial letters of
abbreviations, which are spoken as words.   e.g.   Ufo   (Unidentified Flying
Object)

Anagram - This is where the letters of a word are mixed up to form another
word.
e.g.   toga = goat   deal = lead   With some anagrams the letters are mixed
up so that they don't make a word at all. e.g. kaet = take

Inflection (sometimes spelt **Inflexion**) - This is where the meaning of a word
is changed by adding an affix to the end of it. Plurals are the most common
form of inflection. e.g. girl = girl<u>s</u>   The tense of a word can also be changed
by the addition of an inflection. e.g. talk = talk<u>s</u> / talk<u>ing</u> / talk<u>ed</u> (It can also be
used with comparatives and superlatives).

Malapropisms - This where a word is written or said is mistaken for another
similar sounding or spelt word. e.g. 'he did an experiment in the lavatory' is a
malapropism for 'he did an experiment in the laboratory'. (The term comes
from the character of Mrs. Malaprop in the play *The Rivals* by Sheridan, who
was always getting her words mixed up).

Mnemonic - This refers to the practice of writing or saying phrases as a way
of remembering a particular rule in English. e.g. <u>N</u>aughty <u>E</u>lephants <u>S</u>quirt
<u>W</u>ater is a mnemonic for remembering the points of the compass - <u>N</u>orth
<u>S</u>outh <u>E</u>ast <u>W</u>est.

Portmanteau - This is a word that has been formed by blending some of the letters from two words together. e.g. smoke + fog = smog

Spoonerisms - These are words where the sounds of two words have been swapped over either deliberately or accidentally so that a comical sentence is formed. e.g. 'They bused to catch the rush' which should read 'they rushed to catch the bus'. They are named after an Oxford Don called Dr. Spooner who was always getting his words mixed up.

Zeugma - This is a sentence that contains an extra word or phrase, which applies to the opening words in a different way to the object.
 e.g. We enjoyed the film "Star Wars" and the evening.

Other spelling rules

1) "i before e except after c" is perhaps the most well known spelling rule of all in English, but it doesn't apply to all spellings with those letters in them.
e.g.   'receive' is one word where it works, but some exceptions are 'weird' and 'neighbour'.

2) Words ending in 'i', 'u' or 'v' have an e added to them. e.g. pie, argue, save
Note: there are some words in the English language that <u>do</u> end in 'i', 'u' or 'v', but all these are foreign words which have been accepted into the English language.
e.g.   confetti, spaghetti (Italian), guru (Indian) Molotov (Russian)

3) When using changing nouns which have 'ce' or 'cy' in them into verbs, the 'c' is replaced by an 's'.   e.g. practice = practise

4) If a word ends in 'll', one 'l' is removed when it becomes part of a compound word.
e.g.   help + full = helpful

Silent Letters

Some words contain letters that can't be heard when spoken, although they can be seen in the word. These are called "silent letters". Here is a list of them with examples:

a as in dead	**b** as in dumb	**c** as in scent	**d** as in handsome
e as in minute	**g** as in sign	**gh** as in bough	**h** as in hour
k as in knock	**l** as in yolk	**n** as in autumn	**p** as in psychic
s as in island	**t** as in castle	**u** as in guest	**w** as in writing

Prefixes and Suffixes

Words can have extra beginnings or endings added to them which help to give the basic word - the **root word** - a different meaning.
The letters that are put in front of a word are called **prefixes**. The letters that are put after the word are called **suffixes**. The group name for both these is **affix**.

e.g.   The root word "**press**" can have the prefix **im-** put on the front of it changing it to **impress**. Next it can have the suffix **-ive** added onto the end of it, changing it to **impressive** .

PREFIXES - A prefix can either be a syllable or a small word which is put in front of a root word to change its meaning. Most prefixes that we use today originated from Greek (anti = against), Latin (sub = under) or Old English (mis = wrong). The main prefixes with their meanings and examples are listed below:-

> **a-** (on) - ashore, asleep
> **ab-** (away from) - about, abduct
> **ad-** (to) - adverb, address
> **ante-** (before) - antenatal, antechamber
> **anti-** (opposite, against) - antibiotic, anticlockwise
> **arch-** (chief) - archbishop, arch-enemy
> **auto-** (self) - autograph, automatic
> **be-** (make) - befriend, belief
> **bene-** (make good) - benefit, benevolence
> **bi-** (two of) - bicycle, binoculars
> **bis-** (twice) - bisect, bison
> **circum-** (around) - circumference, circumstance
> **co-** (with) - co-ordinates, co-educational
> **com-** (with) - combine, complete
> **con-** (with) - concentrate, conclude
> **contra-** (against) - contradict, contravene
> **counter-** (against) - counterpart, counterfeit
> **de-** (away) - decompose, descend
> **dec-** (ten) - decimal, decagon
> **dis-** (negative) - disappoint, disgusting
> **em-** (in) - employ, embark
> **en-** (in) - engrave, enclose
> **ex-** (out of) - express, expel
> **for-** (remove) - forget, forbid
> **fore-** (before) - forecast, forehead

homo- (same) - homophone, homonym
hyper- (over) - hyperactive, hypercritical
in- (not) - incredible, inarticulate
in- (in) - inside, in-law
inter- (between) - international, interpreter
mis- (wrong) - mistake, misspell
mono- (one) - monolith, monotonous
non- (not) - nonsense, nonconformist
ob- (against) - obstruct, object
off- (from) - offside, offspring
out- (beyond) - outside, outlaw
over- (over, above) - overdone, overrule
per- (through) - perforate, permit
poly- (many) - polygon, polytechnic
post- (after) - postgraduate, postpone
pre- (before) - previous, prefix
pro- (before) - progress, proceed
quad- (four) - quadrilateral, quadrangle
re- (again) - repeat, return
semi- (half) - semi-final, semi-circle
sub- (under) - submarine, substance
super- (above) - supersonic, superhuman
tele- (from far away) - television, telescope
trans- (across) - transport, transfer
tri- (three) - triangle, tripod
ultra- (beyond) - ultrasound, ultra-violet
un- (not) - unstoppable, unthinkable
un- (reverse) - undo, unravel
uni- (one) - uniform, universe
vice- (in place of) - vice-captain, vice-chancellor
with- (take back) - withhold, wither

Note:- these prefixes make the root word have an opposite meaning

de- e.g. decompose
dis- e.g. disappear
in- e.g. inaudible
un- e.g. unusual

Sometimes there are some words which combine two prefixes:-

e.g. monopoly, autograph, kilogram, forwards, etc.

SUFFIXES - Suffixes are letters or groups of letters that are added to the ends of words which can either change its meaning or to change its part of speech. The main suffixes are listed below:-

-able (these form adjectives from verbs) - capable, enjoyable
-age (these form abstract nouns) - marriage, carriage
-al (these form adjectives) - plural, musical
-an (these form adjectives connected with a place) - urban, Italian
-ance (these form abstract nouns from verbs) - deliverance, endurance
-ant (these are to do with people doing or being things) - servant, ignorant
-ar (these form common nouns) - scholar, pillar
-ar (these form adjectives from nouns) - circular, linear
-ary (these form adjectives connected with types of things) - burglary, primary
-ate (these form verbs which are concerned with change) - populate, inanimate
-ation (these form nouns from verbs) - confirmation, relegation
-crat (these form nouns) - aristocrat, democrat
-cy (these form abstract nouns) - emergency, mercy
-dom (these form abstract nouns) - kingdom, freedom
-ee (these are to do with types of people) - committee, referee,
-eer (these are to do with types of people) - queer, mountaineer
-en (these form verbs to do with changing things) - weaken, thicken
-ence (these form abstract nouns from verbs) - conference, difference
-er (these form nouns connected with people or things) - preacher, streamer
-er (these form comparatives of adjectives) - fatter, harder
-ery (these form adjectives) - flattery, forgery
-ess (these form female nouns) - waitress, lioness
-est (these form superlatives of adjectives) - biggest, coolest
-fold (these are to do with amounts) - tenfold, hundredfold
-ful (these form adjectives from nouns) - fearful, hopeful
-fy (these form verbs to do with changing things) - justify, purify
-gon (these form nouns to do with shapes) - hexagon, polygon
-gram (these form nouns to with metric measures) - kilogram, decagram
-graph (these form nouns to do with writing) - autograph, telegraph
-hood (these form nouns connected with the family) - brotherhood, childhood
-ible (these form adjectives) - incredible, sensible
-ic (these form adjectives) – heroic, pathetic
-ice (these from nouns) - notice, service
-ion (these form abstract nouns) - attention, discussion
-ise (these form endings for verbs) - surprise, practise
-ish (these form adjectives) - mannish, foolish
-ism (these form abstract nouns which show an idea) - socialism, criticism
-ist (these form nouns of people who do certain things) - artist, chemist
-ition (these form nouns) - expedition, competition

-ity (these form nouns) - captivity, equality
-ive (these form adjectives from verbs) - active, impressive
-ize (these form verbs) - capsize, patronize
-less (these form adjectives which mean 'without') - worthless, penniless
-like (these form adjectives which mean the same as) - lifelike, childlike
-ly (these form adverbs from adjectives) - gladly, funnily
-ment (these form abstract nouns) - government, enjoyment
-ness (these form abstract nouns) - darkness, governess
-or (these form nouns to do with occupations) - governor, instructor
-ous (these form adjectives) - spacious, generous
-pathy (these form nouns to do with suffering) - homeopathy, sympathy
-ship (these form abstract nouns to do with situation) - membership, friendship
-sive (these form adjectives from nouns) - aggressive, offensive
-some (these form adjectives to do with how something is) - handsome, tiresome
-th (these from abstract nouns from adjectives or verbs) - health, length
-uble (these form adjectives) - soluble, voluble
-vore (these form nouns to do living things) - carnivore, herbivore
-wise (these from adverbs) - clockwise, otherwise
-xion (these from nouns) - complexion, inflexion
-y (these form adjectives from nouns) - lazy, crazy

All the above suffixes can be said to be **derivational** as they change the type of word it is, such as from a noun to an adverb. The suffixes below are said to be **inflectional** as they change the tense of the word, such as from present tense to past tense:-

-ed - I tried / I had tried
-ing - I was trying

or the quantity of something:-

-es - bus - buses
-s - car - cars

Diminutives

These are words describing small or tiny things. They are usually formed by the addition of a suffix onto the end of a word, (though the prefix, "mini" is also used). Here is a list of the main diminutives and the suffix that is added to them.

-et - cygnet, locket	**-ette** - briquette, cigarette
-kin - lambkin	**-let** - singlet
-ling - duckling, foundling	**-ock** - bullock, hillock

Note:- **mini-** - minibus, miniskirt

Adding Suffixes

When you add suffixes to words that end in a certain letter, there are special rules, which must be followed.

1) If the suffix begins with a consonant and the root word ends in a consonant, they are joined together normally. e.g. boast + ful = boastful

2) If the suffix begins with a vowel (or 'y') and the root word ends in consonant, the consonant needs to be "doubled" before the suffix is added.
e.g.   sit + ing = sitting
This is called **doubling** as you put two of the last letter of the root word in its new form with the suffix added.
Note: This does not apply if the root word ends with two consonants or if it has a long vowel sound. e.g. act + ion = action or clean + er = cleaner

3) If the suffix begins with a vowel and the root word ends in a silent 'e', you take away the 'e'. e.g. take + ing = taking
Note: This does not apply if the suffix begins with 'a' or 'o' and the root word ends with a soft 'ce' or 'ge'.
e.g. service + able = serviceable   or   outrage + ous = outrageous

4) If the suffix begins with a consonant and the root word ends in a silent 'e', you leave the word as it is. e.g. base + ment = basement

5) If the root word ends in 'y' and you want to add 'ing', the 'y' stays on the word.
e.g. steady + ing = steadying

6) If the root word ends in 'y' and has a consonant before it; and you want to add any other suffix apart from 'ing', you change the 'y' to an 'i' or 'i.e.'.
e.g. dirty + er = dirtier   friendly + ness = friendliness

6) If the root word ends in 'y' and has a vowel before it, and you want to add any other suffix apart from 'ing', the 'y' stays on the word. e.g. grey + ing = greying
Note: this does not apply to some one syllable words which end in a vowel + 'y'
e.g. day + ly = daily

7) If you want to add the suffix -ly to a word that ends in 'le' you take away the 'le'.
e.g.   double = doubly

8) If a verb ends in 'c' you add 'k' to it when adding the suffix 'ed', 'er', 'ing' or 'y' to it.
e.g.   panic = panicking

Homophones, Homonyms and Homographs

There is often a lot of confusion between homophones, homonyms and homographs. They all have the prefix, 'homo-' (which is Greek for "the same") but have different endings.

Homophones are words which sound the same but which have a different meaning and are spelt differently - 'phone' meaning 'sound'. Most homophones have two words sounding the same, but in some cases there are three or four words, which can be said to be homophones.

e.g.   buy/by/bye   or   there/their/they're

Here is a list of some of the most common homophones:-

air / heir	arc / ark	ate / eight	ball / bawl	bare / bear
bean / been	berth / birth	blew / blue	border / boarder	
bough / bow	boy / buoy	brake / break	ceiling / sealing	
cereal / serial	coarse / course	dear / deer	die / dye	
faint / feint	fair / fare	flew / flue	fort / fought	
groan / grown	guessed / guest	heal / heel	hear / here	
heard / herd	hole / whole	hour / our	him / hymn	
its /it's	knew / new	knows / nose	leant / lent	
lessen / lesson	mare / mayor	meat / meet	missed / mist	
oh / owe	pair / pear	peace / piece	peer / pier	
queue / cue	rain /reign	ring /wring	road / rode	
sail / sale	scent / sent / cent	sew / so /sow	slay / sleigh	
steal /steel	tail / tale	tire / tyre	way / weigh	
weak / week	weather / whether	which / witch		

Homographs are concerned with words which are spelt the same but which have different meanings <u>or pronunciations</u> - 'graph' meaning 'writing'.

e.g.   He *read* the book   I like to *read* a book

Homonyms are also concerned with words which are spelt the same but which have different meanings - 'nym' meaning 'name'. They <u>also</u> refer to words that are pronounced the same, but which have different meanings. So in this second sense homonyms can be the same as homophones. Most English reference books tend to associate homonyms with homographs, but the reader should be aware of the differences and similarities as stated above.

Here are some of the most common homographs and their meanings:-

arch - a curved piece of a building / a prefix meaning 'main one'
bark - tree skin / noise a dog makes
calf - a baby cow / muscle in your leg
die - to be dead / a dice
even - equal / short for evening
fair - a hair colour / a funfair
grave - a hole for a coffin / serious
howler - a thing that howls / a large mistake (slang)
insert - to put into (verb) / a thing which has been put into something (noun)
jumper - a sweater / a person who jumps
kind - to be nice / a group of people
lead - a metal / a length or rope or leather
match - a game (of football) / a small piece of wood that burns
net - short for netting / a term to do with money
own - to possess something (verb) / your possession (adjective)
pit - a large hole / to use your wits
quad - a four sided area / a prefix meaning four
ram - a male sheep / to push hard
stamp - a small piece of paper used in postage / to strike with your foot
tie - a draw / a piece of cloth you put round your neck
use - to use something (verb) / something that is used (noun)
vice - a grip tool / something very bad
wind - the blowing of air / to turn around something

Compound words

This is when two short words are placed together to make one longer word.

e.g.   black + board = blackboard   part + time = part-time

Some compound words include a hyphen between the two smaller words, though there is no definite rule about this. If the word is more in general use, it tends not to have a hyphen. Nearly all compound words are nouns or adjectives. If the compound word is made up of two adjectives together it usually retains the hyphen.

Some examples of compound words:-

afterwards / barnyard / confuse / download / earthquake / fireman / grandson / heartache / inland / jam-jar / knife-edge / letter-box / madman / nineteen / open-heart / palace / quicksilver / room-mate / something / underneath

Antonyms

Antonyms are words that have **opposite** meanings to each other.

e.g.   buy is the antonym of sell.

As with synonyms, antonyms should be from the same part of speech as each other. Antonyms can be: nouns (pupil/teacher), verbs (open/shut), adjectives (deep/shallow) or adverbs (quickly/slowly).

There are over 400 pairs of antonyms in the English language. Here are some of the more popular ones:-

alive/dead	evening/morning	night/day
asleep/awake	exit /entrance	north/south
back/front	fair/unfair	open/shut
big/little	fat/thin	plural/singular
black/white	give/take	public/private
bitter/sweet	good/bad	question/answer
cheap/dear	hard/soft	retreat/advance
cold/hot	hot/cold	rich/poor
come/go	inferior/superior	rough/smooth
dirty/clean	junior/senior	soft/hard
dry/wet	land/sea	tiny/massive
early/late	last/first	ugly/beautiful
east/west	low/high	victory/defeat
empty/full	mad/sane	war/peace
end/start	make/destroy	young/old

Note: Some antonyms can be formed by the addition of a prefix: -

e.g.   comfortable / uncomfortable   legal / illegal   moral / immoral

Sometimes the prefix can be changed altogether to form the antonym: -

e.g.   export / import   inside / outside

Sometimes the antonym can be formed by altering the suffix at the end of a word:-

e.g.   The antonym of useful is useless

Note: Some words may have several antonyms:-

e.g.   small could have the antonyms of large, big, huge, great, etc.

Synonyms

Synonyms are words that are the **same** or are **similar** in meaning to other words.

e.g.   fast / quick   drop / fall   strange / odd

They can be nouns, verbs, adjectives or adverbs.

Sometimes synonyms seem to have exactly the same meaning in one context:-

e.g.   The service is the restaurant was fast.
or   The service in the restaurant was quick.

Sometimes only one synonym makes sense if they are used in the same sentence:-

e.g.   The cowboy had a quick-fire sharp-shooter gun. (makes sense)
        The cowboy had a fast-fire sharp-shooter gun. (doesn't make sense)

Note: synonyms always belong to the same part of speech:-

e.g.   minister/clergyman (noun) cheeky/insolent (adjective)
        feel/touch (verb)   rarely/seldom (adverb)

Here are some of the more common synonyms:-

aid/help	feeble/weak	rapid/quick
altitude/height	glance/look	reveal/show
ally/friend	imitate/copy	residence/home
brief/short	insane/mad	roam/wander
bright/shiny	join/unite	scene/sight
broad/wide	let/allow	small/little
cease/stop	minimum/least	stubborn/obstinate
conceal/hide	modern/new	suspend/hang
conclude/end	mute/dumb	terror/fear
courage/bravery	near/close	transparent/clear
difficult/hard	novel/new	unite /join
discuss/debate	opinion/view	vacant/empty
encircle/surround	powerful/strong	wealthy/rich
enormous/massive	profit/gain	wicked/evil
famous/well-known	quantity/amount	yearly/annual

A thesaurus or dictionary is the ideal tool for finding synonyms.

Contractions

This a word that has been formed by two words being shortened by the use of an apostrophe.

e.g.   **Can't** is the contraction of "**can not**."

Contractions are used in everyday speech and in informal pieces of writing. For formal writing however it is best not to use contractions.

Here is a list of all the contractions and the words that they come from.

I'd	=	I had/I would	aren't	=	are not
I'll	=	I will/I shall	can't	=	cannot
I'm	=	I am	couldn't	=	could not
I've	=	I have	didn't	=	did not
you'd	=	you had/you would	doesn't	=	does not
you'll	=	you will/you shall	don't	=	do not
you're	=	you are	hadn't	=	had not
you've	=	you have	hasn't	=	has not
he'd	=	he had/he would	haven't	=	have not
he'll	=	he will/he shall	here's	=	here is
he's	=	he is/he has	isn't	=	is not
she'd	=	she had/she would	mustn't	=	must not
she's	=	she has/she has	needn't	=	need not
she'll	=	she will/she shall	shan't	=	shall not
it'd	=	it had/it would	shouldn't	=	should not
it's	=	it is	that's	=	that is
we'd	=	we had/we would	there's	=	there is
we'll	=	we will/we shall	wasn't	=	was not
we're	=	we are	weren't	=	were not
we've	=	we have	what's	=	what is
they'd	=	they had/they would	won't	=	will not
they'll	=	they will/they shall	wouldn't	=	would not
they're	=	they are			
they've	=	they have			
who'd	=	who had			
who'll	=	who will/who shall			
who're	=	who are			
who's	=	who is	Note: who has	=	whose and NOT
who've	=	who have			

Note: There are some words which over the years have contracted themselves into one word from two, but which do not use an apostrophe:

e.g.   already   everyone   nowadays

French Words

Many words in everyday use in English are French words which have a completely different meaning in French, yet are used regularly in conversation and writing.

e.g.   regime, debut, metropolitan, farce, cliché, grand prix, etc.

In some cases the words have accents above the letter 'e' which indicates that they are not an English word.

American English

There are several English words, which have a slightly different spelling in America than they do in England. Sometimes English writers use these "Americanisms". Here are the main differences:-

English words ending in 'our' are changed to an 'or' ending in American English:
behavior (behaviour), color (colour), favor (favour), favorite (favourite), glamor (glamour), humor (humour), neighbor (neighbour), savior (saviour)

English words ending in 're' are changed to an 'er' ending in American English:
center (centre), kilometer (kilometre), liter (litre), meter (metre), specter (spectre)

Other American English words which change just one letter are:
cozy (cosy), curb (kerb), gray (grey) , pretense (pretence), tire (tyre), traveler (traveller)   program (programme) removes the last two letters.

Some American words might mean something completely different in Britain:
'check' in America means 'cheque' and not to stop or restrain.
'Fall' in America means 'autumn' and not to drop.
'Gas' in America means 'petrol' and not the fuel we use for cookers and fires.

There are several more words which Americans use, which have different names than English ones. Here is a list of the main ones with the English equivalent in brackets:

    apartment (flat),   automobile (car),   cookie (biscuit),
    downtown (city centre)   elevator (lift),   kindergarten (infant school),
    movie (film),   sidewalk (pavement),   truck (lorry)

Remember - If in doubt about how to spell a word, **always use a dictionary**. It can also tell you what the word means, what part of speech it is and in some cases how to pronounce the word and which language it originally comes from.

WRITING

Writing in English isn't just concerned with words but involves all the different topics covered in this directory including spelling, grammar, punctuation and parts of speech. There are many different sorts of writing in English including stories, poetry, letters, accounts, instructions and reports. This section includes details on different sorts of writing as well as terms associated with writing.

Writing can be of two types:- fiction and non-fiction. **Fiction** writing is writing which is made up or invented by the writer. It is not real or true, but may have elements of the truth in it, such as having real places for the setting. Fiction writing includes such things as stories, fables, myths, parables and Science-fiction. **Non-fiction** writing on the other hand is writing which is based on real life and will include information writing such as recipes, instructions, directions, articles about people or things. Newspapers, magazines and textbooks are all sources of non-fiction.

Writing a Story

Writing a story involves lots of different things. Before starting to the write the story you should **plan** what you are going to write about. Rather than having some vague ideas in your head, you should write these down on paper. Your plan should include a list of **key-words** and **key-phrases**. These are important words or phrase in the story which will give the story that something extra which will make it stand out from other stories. Usually you will be given a title by the teacher, which should give you an idea of the story's **theme** or subject. This is what the story is all about. e.g. Is it about Space? or travelling through time? or good versus evil? In its simplest form a story should have a **beginning**, a **middle** and an **ending**. This is gives the story a **sequence** as it follows a particular order.

Next you should think about the **plot**. This is about what happens in the story. How does it start? (the **introduction**). How does it develop? What is the final outcome? Next, where does the action in the story take place? In a forest? in a town? Is it in the present? or the past? or the future? This is the **setting** and is the place or places where the events happen. Next, who are the people in the story? Is it you and your friends? or is it some criminals or robbers? Are they nice people or bad people? The people in a story are called the **characters** and they should have different 'characteristics' such as the way they speak or the way they behave. Are they funny or sad? Are they helpful to other people? or do they do bad things? Use your **imagination** to make the story sound real and exciting.

Finally the story needs to come alive by having two other aspects to it - action and dialogue. **Action** is all the events that happen such as people finding things, people getting lost, people fighting, etc. It helps make the story more interesting. **Dialogue** refers to the conversations people have with each other.

The way a person speaks can give the reader clues about what that person is like and helps the story to come alive. Don't forget speech marks to show that someone is speaking when using dialogue. Most important of all the writer must make sure is that s/he has the correct grammar, punctuation and spelling in the story.

The whole **structure** or way the story is built is also important. Make sure you split the story up into appropriate **paragraphs**. These are groups of sentences that are connected by having the same theme or subject. (The start of a new paragraph should always begin on a new line and go in from the margin slightly). Your final paragraph should sum up the story and have a convincing **conclusion** - that is, does it all end happily or is it a sad ending where someone dies? Once you have finished your story (or any piece of writing for that matter) you should always read through it to check if you have made any mistakes, for instance in spelling or punctuation. If you do all if these, you should be able to write a good, well-written and interesting story.

Writing a letter

There are many different sorts of letters. Most letters can be put into two distinct categories:- formal and informal. A formal letter will usually be to someone you don't know, such as writing to someone to ask for information about something, or complaining to a company about a product that was faulty. An informal letter will probably to someone you know very well like a friend or a relative, such as replying to an invitation to a party, or thanking someone for a present.

What a letter needs
Firstly, a letter needs an **address**. This is the place where you are writing the letter. The address should have the name of the house (if there is one), the number of and name of the street, the name of the village or town where you live, the county and finally the postcode.

Secondly, the **date** is put directly underneath the address. Most people write the date in full. i.e. the number of the day in the month, the name of the month and the year. You can also put the day of the week if you wish. It is not correct English to abbreviate the date. i.e. 13/3/99.

Both the address and date are usually situated in the top right hand corner of the piece of paper you are writing on. You may also wish to add your telephone number. This is usually placed straight after the address and before the date.

You should now write the **greeting**. This is the 'Dear....' part. The addressee - the person you are writing to - is put on the top line. Always begin with the word 'dear' followed by the person's name. If it is someone you know well it is fine to call them by their first name. If not, address them with 'Dear Mr. ....' or 'Dear Mrs. ...' followed by a comma. Remember to leave a **margin** - a small gap or space on both sides of your letter

On the next line start writing the main part of your letter. With a personal letter you should start the next line directly underneath where the line above ended. i.e. to the right of the comma. Remember to split your letter up into paragraphs if it is quite long. Start each paragraph about one or two centimetres in from the margin.

To finish the letter you should sign off with 'Yours sincerely' if it is someone you know or 'Yours faithfully' if it is to someone you don't know. Finally write your own name. Your surname should be included if the person you are writing to doesn't know you.

Business letters vary from personal letters in several ways. Firstly, the address of the person or company you are writing to should be put on the left hand side below the level of your address and before you start writing the letter. Secondly, the addressee should be 'Dear Sir' or 'Dear Madam'. Finally, the ending should be 'Yours faithfully' or 'Yours truly'. Nowadays with most business letters being written on word processors or computers, each paragraph starts at the edge of the margin, rather than going in slightly.

Addressing an envelope
Always start about a third of the way down the envelope so there is enough room to put the stamp in the top right-hand corner. The addressee should be put about a third of the way across the envelope, followed by the address, line by line, including the postcode. In the past, each line tended to start slightly to the right of the line above, but nowadays each line of the address starts directly under the start of the line above.

Postcards
Postcards are used not only to send messages from holiday-makers, but also to enter competitions or to leave messages and reminders to different people. They do not have a greeting as such and the message is usually kept to a minimum.

On the next few pages is a list of some of the main types of writing and writing terms in alphabetical order:-

Acrostic This is a line-by-line piece of writing which uses the initial letters of a word one at a time down the page or in the middle of certain key words.

e.g.	Creature with fur	OR	Scratching
	Always sleeping		Chasing
	Terrorises mice		Waiting

Address Most people think of an address as being the place where you live. This is one form of address, but an address can also be a speech by a person such as a priest to a congregation in a church, or by a politician to an audience in a hall.

Advertisements These can be written pieces of information about a product that someone is hoping to sell to the person reading the information, usually in a newspaper or magazine. Advertisements can also be short films on television or at the cinema, which are doing the same thing. These are called 'adverts' for short, or 'commercials'.

Anecdote This is can either be a funny or a serious short story that is used by a writer or speaker to get across a message to his audience.

Appendix This is an extra section of writing which a writer adds onto a piece of writing which s/he did not think was necessary to be included in the main text.

Audience In writing these are the people you are writing your story for - your readers. In a theatre, these are the people who come to watch a play or be entertained by some singers, etc.

Autobiography This is the life story of someone written by the person himself or herself. Usually it is written in the first person, "I did this, then I went to...".

Biography The life story of a person written by someone who is not the subject of the book. Usually it is written in the third person. e.g. "He did this...".

Blurb This refers to the contents of a book and is designed to give a quick overall view of what a particular book is all about. It is usually found on the back cover of a book.

Commentary This is a book or extended piece of writing which gives detailed information about another piece of writing, such as a novel, a book of the Bible, a film, or a poem. It is designed to help the reader understand or comprehend the text more fully.

Composition
This is an old fashioned word which is sometimes used to describe a piece of writing such as an essay, a story, an account or some other piece of continuous writing.

Contents This is a list of the main titles or headings that the reader will come across as he reads a book. It is put at the beginning of the book before the main text starts.

Correspondence This is where two different pieces of information or writing are matched up and placed together.

Definition This is what a word actually means. Definitions of words can be found in a dictionary, which aims to make clear what a word means. Nouns, adjectives and adverbs can all have definitions of them.

Description This is a piece of writing which tells you what something looks like or how something happened. It can be as short as one sentence or as long as several paragraphs. e.g. The Police took a description of what happened from the witness.

Dialogue This refers to the conversation between two people or groups of people. It can either be spoken or written language.

Editorial In a newspaper or a magazine, an 'editorial' is usually a short piece of writing in which the editor gives his or her opinion about some current topic which is in the news. Alternatively, it can be an introduction to the rest of the magazine.

Epitaph This is the writing that is found on a tombstone, which gives some information about the deceased person or uses some words from the Bible or other book. e.g. "He lived his life to the full" OR "She was taken from this life far too soon".

Essay This is an extended piece of writing where the writer will write about his or her views and ideas on a specific subject. It could be a story (fiction) or it could be an report about a football match (non-fiction).

Eulogy This can either be in the form of a speech or in a piece of writing and is designed to praise a person's life or achievements. It is sometimes directed towards someone who has recently died.

Fable This is a short story, which is designed to show the reader a moral or lesson in life, which should be learnt. Usually it involves animals or natural things (such as trees or the wind). The most famous collection of fables is "Aesop's Fables" from Ancient Greece.

Fairy Tale These are children's stories which involve magic and creatures like fairies, witches, goblins, elves, etc. They usually involve some sort of confrontation between good and evil, in which good always wins. They usually start with the words, "Once upon a time ..." and end with the words, "and they all lived happily ever after". e.g. Cinderella or Red Riding Hood are well known fairy tales. Some fairy tales are re-enacted over the Christmas season as pantomimes.

Fantasy This is writing which is completely made up which is dependant on the writer's imagination about something happening. It could involve magic as in fairy tales, or it could involve futuristic inventions such as in Science fiction.

Footnote This is a piece of extra information that the writer adds to the bottom of a page of writing for the reader to see apart from the main text.

Glossary This is a list of words or terms and their meanings from a text which the reader may be unfamiliar with.

Index This is a list of the main words in a piece of writing or a book. They are placed in alphabetical order and put at the end of the book/piece of writing.

Information text This is a piece of writing which has the purpose of giving information about a subject to the reader. It could be a **report** on a news item, or an **explanation** about how something occurred.

Instruction text This is a piece of writing which has the purpose of instructing the reader about how to do something such as conducting a Science experiment.

Jargon This refers to the language that is used by a particular group of people, which only they can understand, such as a group of scientists.

Legend This can be one of two things. Firstly, it refers to an old story which is probably based on a true heroic character, but which has been changed in parts over the years, so that the truth is not exactly as it happened. Secondly, it can refer to information on a map such as the words and symbols.

Media These are all the different types of communications there are which give out words in some form or other. i.e. newspapers, magazines, television, radio, the Internet, etc.

Messages These are short pieces of information sent by one person to another giving details about something. It could be on paper; by telephone or fax; or it could be on the computer, via e-mails. Sometimes messages can be put inside cards remembering a birthday, Christmas or an anniversary.

Monologue This can be a story, which is told in the first person singular by one person alone, or it can be a person in a group dominating the conversation.

Myth This is a very old story concerning gods or heroes from ancient times, which explains why something has happened or why something exists in the world. e.g. The Tower Of Babel story in the Old Testament explains how different languages came into being.

Narrative Text This is a piece of writing which recounts an event, which has happened, so the audience learns about the events in chronological order.

Narrator This is the name given to the person who tells a story or introduces a play as he or she 'narrates' events in the story/play.

Non-chronological text This is similar to narrative text but it does not follow a chronological sequence. Instead it will show certain characteristics about the information it is providing. e.g. An account about an animal might show details of its habitat, its food, its habits, its young, etc.

Novel This is a long story that has been put into book form. e.g. Great Expectations by Charles Dickens. (A **novelist** is the person who writes novels).

Obituary A piece of prose in a newspaper or magazine which gives details of the life of a person who has recently died, mentioning their main achievements.

Palindrome This is a word or phrase that can be written back to front and still be the same. e.g. dad, mum, madam, etc.

Parable This is a story like a fable, which gives out a lesson or moral to the listener. e.g. In the Gospels of the New Testament, Jesus told many parables.

Parody This is a story or a poem where the writer changes a person's character so that it is copied or imitated to such an extreme that it becomes funny.

Persuasive Text This is where a writer puts forward a point of view he feels strongly about in his writing. In it he might use **arguments** as well as evidence, which explain why he holds a certain view, in order to 'persuade' the reader.

Play This is a story, which is acted out on a stage as **drama** using direct speech.

Prose This is writing which does not follow the rules of poetry or drama in that it does not have a rhyme, a rhythm or verses.

Proverb This is a short saying that is designed to give a warning or advice to the listener. Often they rhyme. e.g. 'when the cat's away, the mice will play'. They are usually easy to remember, due to their brevity. e.g. 'more haste, less speed'. Many of them are thousands of years old and contain wisdom from ancient writers that is timeless. e.g. There is a whole book in the Old Testament called 'Proverbs' which is completely made up of proverbs. Proverbs may have a literal meaning, but they have a figurative meaning as well. e.g. 'Don't put all your eggs in one basket' is really saying, 'Don't put all your money in one place, in case it gets stolen'.

Pun This is a play on words where words are used which sound the same, but which have a different meaning. e.g. My father told me the doctor will heel me, when all I wanted was shoe-mender! Most puns use homonyms to achieve their effect as in the above example. They are often used in newspaper headlines when there is a funny story to report.

Recipes These are instructions on how to prepare and cook food. A recipe will begin with a list of ingredients needed, followed by the method, stage by stage, so the food will come out exactly as it should. Recipes are similar in form to science experiment instructions where the same sorts of processes are involved.

Recount Text This is writing about either a fictitious event such as a ghost story or a non-fictional account about an event that has happened. It is written from the perspective of someone who has been at the event and is retelling events as they happened stage by stage.

Reference Text This is writing where the writer is giving out detailed information about a particular topic, so that the reader will learn about this topic. e.g. a detailed description of the life cycle of a frog would be such a text. To get such information, the writer would look for details in a **reference book**.

Riddle This is a type of puzzle, which asks the reader to solve a question that the writer is asking. A lot of jokes take this form. e.g. 'Why did the chicken cross the road? To get to the other side!' Most, but not all riddles have some sort of humour in them and many take the form of puns.

Story Board This is a series of pictures, which filmmakers use to show the plot of the film. in the classroom teachers can use story boards to help children plan their stories or to use as a piece of comprehension. Popular comics use storyboards in their layout.

Summary This is a short summing up of a story or other text, which mentions its main points in a few sentences.

Tall Story This is a story where the events and/or characters are highly exaggerated. They became popular as a literary form through the writings of Baron Munchhausen.

Text This is any kind of writing, which is used to communicate ideas or information.

Tongue-twister This is a saying which is so difficult to say that it is as if the tongue gets twisted as you attempt to say it. e.g. 'Peter Piper picked a pickled pepper'...

POETRY

Poetry is writing which usually has <u>verses</u> or sections and has a <u>rhythm</u>. **Rhythm** is the number of **beats** on a line so that when read aloud you get an accent or emphasis on certain words. This is often known as the **metre** of a poem. Each part of the metre is made up of a **foot**, which in turn is made up of one or more syllables.

Some, but not all poetry has a <u>rhyme</u> as well. **Rhyme** is where the words at the end of two lines have the same sound or vowel phoneme. e.g. blue/screw chair/square. Rhyming words aren't always spelt the same, as the two examples show. Poetry can be funny - as in limericks or lampoons. It can also be serious and show a range of emotions, which are designed to affect the reader - as in poems by such well-known writers as Shakespeare, Wordsworth and Betjemen.

When a **poem** is written it is said to be **verse** if it has lines which are a certain length and which have a metre or rhythm. Usually each line should begin with a capital letter and the words at the end of each line may rhyme. Verse can also refer to the parts or divisions of a piece of poetry. A verse is usually 4, 6 or 8 lines long and is also called a stanza (see below). Poetry has many different forms and many special words associated with it. Many of these are set out below.

Ballad This is a poem or a song, which tells the story of something. The verses are usually short and rhyme. e.g. "The Ballad of Bonnie and Clyde".

Blank Verse This is poetry which doesn't rhyme but which has a rhythm and a metre. It can be in the form of iambic pentameter - this is a short syllable followed by a long one.

Calligram This is a poem in which the calligraphy - the type and size of the writing is a reflection of what the poem is all about.

e.g.   The water dr

                ip

                p

                ed   down from the tap.

Cinquain This is a poem, which was invented by an American poet called Adelaide Crapsey, which is made up of five lines in the sequence of 2, 4, 6, 8, 2 and has 22 syllables in its five lines.

Clerihew This is a four lined poem in comic form named after its creator, E. Clerihew Bentley. It has two rhyming couplets with the first line being the name of the subject of the poem.

Concrete poem This is a poem where the words are laid out in such a way as to show a characteristic of the subject. They are similar in form to a shape poem - see below.

Couplet This is two lines of poetry next to each other, which may rhyme or have the same number of syllables.

Doggerel This is verse which may rhyme but is written in such a simple way that it is not proper poetry. e.g. She ate the cake which took me ages to bake. Oh how my heart aches!

Elegy This is a poem or a song which is usually about someone who has died.
e.g.   "Gray's Elegy" is a well known example of an elegy.

Epic This is a poem (or a story) about a legendary character who is usually a national hero. e.g. "The Epic of Gilgamesh" tells the story of the great flood.

Free verse This refers to poetry which doesn't always have a rhythm or a rhyme.

Haiku A Haiku is a Japanese poem, which has just three lines. The first line has five syllables, the second line has seven syllables and the third line has five syllables.

e.g.   Lonely man, alone
            Sitting under the hot sun
            Thinking where he is

Half-rhyme These are words that do not completely rhyme.
            e.g.   gone/gun,   one/won

Internal rhyme This refers to words which rhyme inside one line of poetry.
            e.g. He waited for his flat-mate to give him eight dates.

Jingle This is usually a one or two-line poem, which is designed to attract the reader's or listener's attention in order to get a message across. Jingles are often used on the radio to sell a product.

Kenning This is an Old English (Or Norse) two word form, which is used to describe something without naming that thing. e.g. a house might be called 'dwelling place', whilst a cow might be called 'milk giver'.

Lampoon This is a comic verse whose purpose is to mock at or make fun of someone in a hurtful way.

Limerick This is a funny or comic verse consisting of five lines with eight syllables in the first, second and fifth lines and six syllables in the fourth and fifth lines. The first, second and fifth lines have the same rhyme, whilst the third and fourth lines have a different rhyme. Usually the fifth line is almost the same as the first line as in the limerick below:-

e.g.   These was once a man from Blackpool,
           Who drank a cup full of brown gruel.
           He asked, "What have I drunk?"
           This smells just like a skunk.
           That silly old man from Blackpool

Limericks are sometimes known as **joke poems**. The person who is remembered for making the limerick well known is Edward Lear. (See nonsense verse below).

Lullaby This is a song which is usually sung to a baby or young child which is designed to send them to sleep by its gentle rocking beat.

Narrative poem This is a poem that tells a story an. e.g. "The Pied Piper of Hamelin" is a famous narrative poem.

Nonsense verse Like the limerick, Edward Lear is remembered for making nonsense verse popular. This is where the poem rhymes but its content doesn't make sense, although it may be funny to the reader. e.g. Jabberwocky by Lewis Carroll is a good example of nonsense verse.

Ode This is a poem which is usually written in the second person singular - 'you' - as it is addressing the person it is written to. It may not have a rhyme or a rhythm pattern and its language can be strange. It is a poem, which might be sung.

Renga This is where several Haiku (the Japanese three line poem) are linked to each other by two lines consisting of seven syllables.

Shape poem This is a poem where the way the words are laid out is a reflection of the subject matter in the poem.

Sonnet This is poem which has fourteen lines with a distinct rhyme scheme.

Stanza This refers to several lines or a verse of poetry, which are repeated at regular intervals throughout the poem.

Tanka This is a Japanese poem which has five lines and thirty-one syllables which are arranged in the pattern of 5, 7, 5, 7, 7 syllables. It is similar to the haiku but has two extra lines, which reflect the mood of the poem.

COMPREHENSION

Comprehension is the <u>understanding</u> of the English language. It can also be a piece of text where a student has to answer certain questions based on the text. The type of text used for comprehension can be one of several different types. It could be a narrative, which is describing a particular scene; it could be a story with dialogue in it; it could be a poem; or it could be a piece of information such as a chart, timetable of recipe which the student has to comprehend. The student will then have to read the text and answer questions on the text. The answers could be straightforward sentences, a single word or a multiple-choice answer, where the student must choose one answer from several possibilities. In most cases the student will have to show an understanding of the text, but s/he may also have to give an **opinion** on certain aspects of the text. A sample piece of comprehension is set out below which would be suitable for a child aged 9 - 10 (middle Juniors) to answer. The answers are then set out after the passage with useful hints for answering a piece of comprehension effectively.

The Stranger

The man in the dark overcoat looked rather strange to the children. Sam and his sister, Eloise were staying at a holiday cottage on the Welsh island of Anglesey for their summer holiday. Their parents, Steve and Jackie Turner had taken them to the nearby town of Bangor for the day. They had visited the Cathedral and were looking around the shops when they came across the stranger in the dark overcoat, standing in the doorway of an empty shop. He had a peaked cap over his black hair and he seemed to be in pain.

"I wonder what he's doing, standing there?" enquired Sam in a quiet voice, so that the man would not hear.

"I don't know," replied his sister. "He doesn't look particularly friendly".

"Hurry up!" shouted their father, a few feet further on. "It looks like it's going to rain soon".

With that the Turner family went into a local cafe for a cup of tea and some cakes, just as it started to rain. A few minutes later as they were pouring out their tea, Eloise saw the stranger go past. He was walking with a definite limp and his face seemed to be looking towards the ground.

"Eloise!" shouted her mother. "Your tea's getting cold".

"Sorry mum," replied Eloise, her mind wrapped up in thoughts about the stranger.

By the time the family had finished their tea and cakes, it had stopped raining. Large puddles of rainwater were everywhere. They were making their way back to the car park when they heard a commotion ahead.

A few metres ahead they could see the stranger being held by two policemen. He was struggling and shouting something out in a language they couldn't understand. Several people were looking at what was going on. He was being put into a police van just as the Turner's arrived at the car park.

"I wonder what all that was about?" remarked Dad as he opened the car.

"No doubt it'll be in the local newspaper tomorrow," replied Mum.

Hints for answering comprehension passages effectively: -

Firstly, always read through the passage at least once, making sure that you understand what the passage is about; who the main characters are; where the action takes place and noticing any unusual or difficult to understand words or phrases. Do not start answering the questions until you have read through the passage or you might make some silly mistakes.

Secondly, if there are words that you do not know the meaning of, see if you can understand them by their **context**. i.e. what they mean in the whole sentence.

Thirdly, make sure that you answer the questions with full sentences. Never start an answer with the word "because" or put a one-word answer. Use some of the words in the question in your answer. (See the examples below)

Fourthly, try and answer all the questions if at all possible. If you are not sure what the answer is, don't waste time trying to write an answer. Leave a gap and go onto the next question. If you have enough time, come back to the question you missed out.

Finally, always check through what you have written, in case you have made any mistakes.

Questions and answers to "The Stranger" comprehension:-

1)   Q. What was the name of the island on which the Turner family were staying?
      A. The island was called Anglesey

2)   Q. What building in Bangor had the family already visited that day?
      A. The family had already visited the Cathedral in Bangor that day.

3)   Q. Apart from the overcoat, what was the Stranger wearing?
      A. The passage tells us that he was wearing a peaked cap.

4)   Q. Where did the family go after seeing the stranger?
           a) The Cathedral   b) The park   c) A cafe   d) The Police station
      A. (c) The family went to the cafe.

5)   Q. What part of speech is "definite" (line 15)?
      A. "Definite" is an adjective.

6)   Q. What does the word "commotion" mean (line 22)?
           a) movement   b) anger   c) jumping   d) disturbance
      A.. The word "commotion" means disturbance.

7)   Q. What is the literary term for "struggling and shouting something. . ?"
      A. The literary term for this is alliteration.

8)   Q. Whereabouts was the Turner family when all this was happening?
      A. The Turner family was making their way back to the car park.

9)   Q. What finally happened to the stranger?
      A. He was put in a police van OR The stranger was arrested.

10) Q. Write in your own words who you think the Stranger was.
      A. Any sensible and imaginative answer - e.g. I think that the stranger was an escaped prisoner.

OTHER INFORMATION

There are many useful books for finding out information about the English language. Below is a list of the most important **reference books** and their uses. This is followed by some other pieces of information, which is useful for the primary School child.

A **Dictionary** is the most important reference book for the English language. It tells you how to spell a word correctly and what that word means. It also tells you what part of speech a word is and which language it may have come from.

A **Thesaurus** is different to a dictionary in that it puts words into groups of similar meanings and word families. It is useful for finding a different way of saying something. e.g. Instead of saying "I liked ...", you could use the words: loved, appreciated, admired, was fond of, worshipped, etc.

A **Lexicon** is a special sort of dictionary that specialises in Greek, Hebrew and Arabic originated words.

An **Encyclopaedia** gives information on one particular subject such as animals, sports etc., or an all round knowledge such as Science, Geography, Music, History, etc.

Other sources of information, which can be helpful to a Primary school pupil, include **newspapers**, **magazines**, **timetables**, **catalogues**, **directories**, **atlases**, and **textbooks** on a particular subject. All these books can be found in a **library**. A more recent source of information is the Internet which people "surf" to find information on every topic under the sun.

Below are some other aspects of the English language (including lists of words), which a Primary School child will find useful.

Analogies
This is where one thing is similar to another thing, which is connected in some way to a more familiar thing. e.g. fin is to fish as wing is to bird. The fin is connected to the fish, as it is a part of its body that helps it move. A similar analogy would be the wing connected to the bird as that too helps it to move.

Colours
The primary colours are: blue red yellow white and black. All other colours can be formed by mixing these colours in different combinations. Here is a list of all the other principal colours: green purple pink violet gold bronze silver turquoise scarlet orange grey beige cream buff chestnut olive pearl

Some colours are prefaced by nouns to say what particular shade they are:

e.g.   pea-green, blood-red, coal-black, sky-blue, snow-white, etc.

Abbreviations
An abbreviation is a word that has been shortened to its initial letter or sound. There are two sorts of abbreviations:-

1)   Where a word (sometimes in Latin) has been shortened to its first few letters. "e.g." is short for "exempli gratia". In English this means "for example".

2)   Where a name of an organisation has been shortened to the first letters of each of the words in its name. e.g. British Broadcasting Corporation is BBC

Note: It is now common practice for abbreviations using capital letters to miss out the full stops after each letter. lower case letters tend to keep the capital letter.

Here is a list of the main abbreviations, which are useful for a primary school child:

AA - Automobile Association AD - *Anno Domini* (Latin for "In The Year of our Lord") adj. - adjective adv. - adverb   AIDS - Acquired Immune Deficiency Syndrome am - *ante meridiem* (before noon) Aug. - August BA - Bachelor of Arts   BASIC - Beginners' All-purpose Symbolic Instruction Code   BBC - British Broadcasting Corporation Br. - British BST - British Summer Time C - Centigrade c. - *circa* (about) Cantab. - of Cambridge Co. - company/county d. - died dept. - department   Dr - Doctor   D.V. - *Deo volente* (God willing) Ed. - editor/edited by   EEC - European Economic Community esp. - especially F - Fahrenheit FA - Football Association Fr. - Father (put before a priest's name) GB - Great Britain g - gram HMS - Her/His Majesty's Ship Hon. - Honourable i.e. - *id est* (that is) IOU - I owe you   JP - Justice of the Peace Kt. - Knight l - litre Ltd - Limited m - married/metre   MA - Master of Arts m.p.h. - miles per hour NATO - North Atlantic Treaty Organisation op. - *opus* (work) Oxon. - of Oxford p.a. - *per annum* (each year) p.m. - *post meridiem* (after midday) PE - Physical Education pop. - population Pte. - Private QC - Queen's Counsel RAC - Royal Automobile Club Rev. - Reverend (put before a vicar's name) sec. - second SOS - Save Our Souls St. - Saint/street TV - Television UK - United Kingdom UNO - United Nations Organisation VC - Victoria Cross w.c. - water closet (toilet) wt. - weight Xmas - Christmas yr. - year Zech. - Zechariah

Days of the week (abbreviations in brackets)
Sunday   (Sun),   Monday   (Mon),   Tuesday   (Tue),   Wednesday   (Wed), Thursday (Thu),   Friday (Fri),   Saturday (Sat).

Months of the year (abbreviations in brackets)
January (Jan), February (Feb), March (Mar), April (Apr), May (May), June (Jun), July (Jul), August (Aug), September (Sep), October (Oct), November (Nov), December (Dec).

Numbers (Cardinal)

one, two, three, four, five, fix, seven, eight, nine, ten, eleven, twelve, thirteen, fourteen, fifteen, sixteen, seventeen, eighteen, nineteen, twenty, thirty, forty, fifty, sixty, seventy, eighty, ninety, one hundred, one thousand, one million.

Numbers (Ordinal)

first, second, third, fourth, fifth, sixth, seventh, eighth, ninth, tenth, eleventh, twelfth, thirteenth, fourteenth, fifteenth, sixteenth, seventeenth, eighteenth, nineteenth, twentieth, twenty-first, thirtieth, fortieth, fiftieth, sixtieth, seventieth, eightieth, ninetieth, hundredth, thousandth, millionth.

Movements

Certain animals and other objects move in certain ways. There are special verbs for these movements. Some of them are set out below:

bull - charges / frog - leaps / horse - gallops / mouse - scampers / duck - waddles / eagle - swoops / seagull - glides / the tide - ebbs and flows / smoke - billows

Sounds

As with movements, some animals and objects make certain sounds. Here are some of the more important examples:

cat - meows / dog - barks / donkey - brays / lamb - bleats / duck - quacks / pigeon - coos / horse - neighs / the wind - whistles or howls / brakes - screech

Containers

In English certain objects go with certain containers which hold them.

e.g. a bottle of milk or a carton of cream. Here are some other examples:

bag - sugar / barrel - beer / bottle - wine / bowl - cereal / envelope - letter / jar - jam / hamper - picnic / lunch-box - sandwiches / punnet - strawberries / sack - potatoes / tank - petrol / vase - flowers

Senses

Sight (eyes), Smell (nose), Hearing (ears), Taste (tongue), Touch (fingers).

Occupations

Athlete, Artist, Barber, Butcher, Carpenter, Chauffeur, Chemist, Computer Technician, Decorator, Dentist, Detective, Doctor, Engineer, Farmer, Glazier, Grocer, Joiner, Journalist, Mechanic, Miner, Newsagent, Nurse, Optician, Plumber, Policeman, Postman, Sailor, Soldier, Surgeon, Tailor, Teacher, Vet.

Buildings

Brewery, Bus Station, Cathedral, Church, Cinema, Court, Factory, Flats, Hospital, House, Mosque, Office Block, Police Station, Prison, Railway Station, School, Shop, Stadium, Supermarket, Synagogue, Temple, Theatre.

INDEX